Lessons Learned Along the Way:

Survival Tips for School Leaders

.

DENNIS KELLY

American Association of School Administrators
1801 N. Moore St.
Arlington, VA 22209
(703) 875-0748
http://www.aasa.org

EXECUTIVE DIRECTOR: Paul D. Houston
DEPUTY EXECUTIVE DIRECTOR: E. Joseph Schneider
EDITOR: Ginger R. O'Neil, GRO Communications
DESIGNER: Jim McGinnis, Mac Designs

Printed in the United States of America.

AASA Stock Number: 236-008
ISBN: 0-87652-236-3
Library of Congress Catalog Card Number: 98-74989

To order additional copies, call AASA's Order Fulfillment Department at 1-888-782-2272 (PUB-AASA) or, in Maryland, call 1-301-617-7802.

Dedication

To my parents,
Marion and Gerald Kelly,
my first and best teachers

■

The author's proceeds from the sale of this book will be
donated to the Dennis G. Kelly Scholarship Fund at
University High School in Normal, Illinois.

Lessons Learned Along the Way: Survival Tips for School Leaders

S U R V I V A L   T I P S   A - Z
(W E L L ,   A L M O S T *)

V

*Editor's Note: Though the lack of a title for every letter might look like an example of laziness on our parts, we assure you that it was a conscious decision. After much debate, we decided that it is impossible to ever learn or share all of the leadership lessons needed by successful school leaders. So, though we are sharing many great lessons with you, the missing letters represent the learning that you will certainly need to continue to do on your own. The fact that those letters include the ever-hard-to-use Q, V, X, and Z is purely coincidental. Really.

VIII

Introduction

It was going to be a long Board meeting. We had recently made a major change in the attendance policy for the school district—one of those magical decisions that galvanized the entire community. They all hated it and they were poised to attack.

As we entered the communications portion of the Board meeting, a long line of speakers waited in front of an open microphone. Not one of them was smiling. I turned to the Board president and whispered, "Isn't this exciting? Tonight we'll find out how good we are at dodging bullets. Don't you just love your job?"

Being a leader in today's schools is definitely challenging. It can be an emotional roller coaster ride that is unpredictable, exhilarating, depressing, exciting, and stressful. For too many administrators, the ride is all too brief. One minute the community is giving you a plaque; the next minute they're interviewing your replacement.

What you need to know to survive as a leader in our schools can't be learned in a single graduate course or from reading a textbook. You develop leadership skills by leading and by learning from your mistakes. In my career, I have learned more from disasters than from victories. And I have also learned from other people's mistakes. After reading this book, you will understand why it is possible to learn more when you aren't smiling and why when bad things happen your learning curve improves dramatically.

This book is an informal history of my experiences during 20 years in administration and some of the hard lessons I've learned along the way. The stories are me talking aloud to myself or retelling someone else's tale. The collective picture is what I see when I look back over those 20 years. These are stories of common sense, nonsense, inspiration, and dismal failures. They happen to all of us.

The journeys I describe aren't all pleasant walks in the park. They reflect what happens in the trenches, not someone's idea of what should happen in a perfect world. But for every nightmare, there is at least one moment of joy and exhilaration.

The overall tone of this book might not be all smiles, but it's honest. I have tried to avoid rewriting your favorite textbook or a research-based thesis with endless footnotes, and this certainly isn't an educational leadership cookbook. I could never personally find enough of the ingredients to follow anyone else's recipe.

Being a leader isn't simple. Don't waste your time looking for a magic formula for success. There are no "12 Steps to Being a Successful Leader." There is no rule book or manual. Leadership is a combination of using your head and listening to your heart. The most common element is also the most unpredictable—people. Leadership is all about human relationships and using human values to solve problems and help others.

I hope this book helps you recognize a few of the land mines before you step on them. I have already made enough mistakes in my career for at least two people. If you can learn from my mistakes, maybe you can minimize the number you will make. And if my stories can keep you from losing a night's sleep, or worse, losing your job, I will consider the time I've spent writing worthwhile.

A good team will beat a great player every time

Michael Jordan was the premier player in the NBA for a number of years, but for much of his early career the Chicago Bulls couldn't win a championship. Even with the greatest player in the history of the game, the Bulls were unable to consistently beat the best teams. It wasn't until the Bulls developed talent like Scottie Pippen, Horace Grant, and Toni Kukoc to compliment their superstar that they were able to win a record number of consecutive NBA championships.

Michael Jordan couldn't do it alone and neither can you. Even the best leaders will fail if they have a weak supporting cast or try to do too much themselves. Put your best people in the key spots in your schools. Develop the talents of those around you. Involve people in making important decisions. Delegate responsibilities and hold people accountable. Then get out of the way and let people do their jobs.

■

1

Admitting your mistakes is easier (and smarter) than trying to cover them up

Frank Lloyd Wright said, "The physician can bury his mistakes, but the architect can only advise his client to plant vines." Educators can't their bury clients or plant vines, so we must rely instead on telling the truth.

One of my colleagues was responsible for developing and monitoring his school's staffing plan. It was a huge school and a complex job. Halfway through the year, he discovered a mistake in calculating positions for the math and science departments. What should he do? Should he make minor adjustments in all of the numbers to balance out the mistake? Should he say nothing and hope his error might go undetected? Should he tell the superintendent? How would the Board react?

Fortunately, he came into my office and shared the problem. I told him to directly approach the Board, explain the mistake and how he would prevent it from happening again, beg their forgiveness, and then fall on his sword.

"They won't fire you for making one small mistake," I said, "but they will fire you for lying to them." Mistakes and secrets are never kept quiet for long.

No one expects you to be perfect, not a supervisor or the Board of Education. Your whole relationship with your board and people is built upon trust and honesty, and truth is a pretty fragile thing. Once you begin to take liberties with it, it quickly dies.

■

AMERICAN ASSOCIATION OF SCHOOL ADMINISTRATORS

All that annoys isn't useless

It was definitely a full moon night. They were out there in big numbers. The mother of the cheerleader who didn't make the squad because she couldn't do a back flip. The parents of a student who had been dropped from classes for nonattendance; he wasn't with them. The small business owner who wanted to complain about our high tax rate and the illiterate help he had been hiring. The ex-police officer who wanted us to place metal detectors in all the school buildings. And the retiree who would lecture us about the glory days of education in the 1950s.

They weren't on the published agenda, but they would surely speak their piece, and at least one of them would make the papers in the morning in a more prominent place than the details of our $16,000,000 building plan.

These are the critics of public education. And there are lots of them. They all deeply care about an issue that's probably not part of your annual goals. But that doesn't matter. You still need to listen to them and treat them with respect because occasionally, amidst the tom-foolery and nonsense, you will hear bits of wisdom and insights that will make your patience a good investment. And above all, you must remember that these people are paying an important person's salary—yours.

■

A threat with an empty gun
soon loses its impact

We were into the second hour of our family vacation and my third threat. I was already exasperated with my three children.

"That's it. I have had more than enough of your bickering and constant fighting. If I hear one more sound coming from the back seat, I am stopping the car and dropping off the guilty party in the ditch."

Immediately an image of my 4-year-old hitch-hiking by the side of the busy interstate appeared in my head. This might not enhance my image in the community. It wasn't the first time I had made an empty threat as a father. And it surely wouldn't be the last.

I do the same thing at work. And so might you. Our work environments are filled with empty threats; some of them in writing and some of them verbal. And they almost never work.

We can try to threaten people with written contracts we almost would never enforce, with rules and regulations in handbooks no one reads, and by trying to enforce federal and state regulations that no one understands. We naively want to believe that there is a direct relationship between the number of rules and the quality of life. And the more punitive the rules, the better. But trying to legislate morality has never worked in Washington, D.C., or in our schools.

Threats and rules only work to the degree they can be enforced. The really effective organizations and schools have only a few basic rules that people understand, support, and follow. How many do you have?

■

Be careful what you wish for

It's late Friday afternoon. The building is almost empty and there aren't many cars left in the parking lot. Across the street, the lights are coming on. It's time to go home. Somewhere there is a warm supper waiting for me.

It's been a good week. Not many battles, and no blood shed. No controversial issues or tough decisions, just routine stuff. My desk is almost clear. There is no stack of blue phone slips in the corner. All my letters have been written.

It's been a successful, peaceful week. I silently wish for a career filled with many, many such weeks. But am I wishing for too much of the wrong thing? Too many "successful weeks" strung together in a row can kill a career and stop a school in its tracks. While there is great comfort in the routine and the predictable, we grow by going beyond the status quo. Too many schools fall into the trap of trying to preserve the status quo. They will do anything to avoid conflict and ensure peace and tranquillity. But change by its very nature breeds conflict and controversy. It can be unsettling and disturbing, but it is necessary.

Learn to enjoy the peaceful weeks when they occur, but don't strive for too many of them. Cemeteries have caretakers. Schools need leaders.

■

"Because he takes no credit, credit never leaves him"

It was a Board meeting that we lovingly refer to as "a dog-and-pony show." We were highlighting two of our most successful academic programs and the staff who ran them. I sat in the background, answered a few minor questions, and enjoyed the evening. At the end of the two presentations, I publicly recognized the staff members' hard work and professionalism.

After the meeting had ended, several Board and community members approached me. "You should be extremely proud of the excellent programs you have been able to create," they said.

"But I really didn't do anything. Our staff did all the work. They deserve full credit for our success."

"Oh, don't be silly. None of this could have happened without your hard work and leadership. You're being too modest."

"I am not being modest; I'm telling you the truth. I don't deserve the credit," I protested. But they ignored my objections and continued to lavish praise on me all the way out into the parking lot. I went home happy, but feeling a little guilty at their misplaced praise.

One of the ironies of being a leader is there is no way you can bring credit to yourself for doing a job well without it appearing to be a self-serving power play, but the more you recognize others in the organization, the more positively it reflects back on you.

As the Chinese philosopher Lao-Tzu said in the 6th century: "Because he takes no credit, credit never leaves him."

■

Being on top of the organizational chart doesn't necessarily give you the best view

She confronted me somewhere between the cucumbers and broccoli.

"Dr. Kelly, can I bother you for just a minute?" she asked. It seemed like such an innocent request.

"Sure, why not. I can never decide what green vegetables to buy and could use the extra time," I replied, knowing that chance encounters in the produce aisle are never what they seem to be.

Over the next 20 minutes, she relayed to me her anguish over the handling of a fight her son was involved in earlier in the week.

"Surely you have heard all about the fight, Dr. Kelly," she said.

"No. I don't know everything that happens in our school district, and in particular, I didn't know your son was involved in a fight in his 3rd hour English class," I replied honestly.

She was genuinely amazed.

"You didn't know about the fight?" she repeats.

"No, I didn't." I repeat. "But I am sure there is at least one assistant principal who knows all about it and I will have him call you Monday morning with the details."

Despite my appropriate answer, she walks away from me shaking her head, wondering how I could be so far out of the information loop.

Just having your name at the top of the organizational chart doesn't guarantee you will know everything or need to know everything. Indeed, the higher you climb on the organizational chart, the more impossible it becomes to know all of the minutiae. We must all fight the urge to want to know everything. The best strategy is to organize your system so that people know where to go for information and to get their problems solved, and learn to rely on the talent and knowledge of other people in your organization.

■

AMERICAN ASSOCIATION OF SCHOOL ADMINISTRATORS

Be sure you are spending more time solving problems than complaining about them

It was just another early morning staff meeting. We were sitting around a large table drinking coffee and trying to work up the courage to face another day. The topic as usual centered on our perennial problems: micro-management by the Board, the latest grievance from the teachers union, and another case of parental harassment. One of the junior team members raised an interesting question.

"I have been here for two years now. It seems like every week we sit around and whine about the same continuing problems. Has anyone ever tried to do anything to solve these problems or is it enough to just talk about them?"

We looked at him dumbfounded.

"What do you mean solve these problems?" a veteran replied.

"Well, let's take the Board doing too much micro-managing. Why are they micro-managing? In what areas are they interfering with operations? Have we ever offered a workshop on the roles and responsibilities of board members? Why haven't we sat down with them and gone through a number of different situations to give them ideas on how they can be more effective as Board members?"

There was silence at the table. We had all fallen into the habit of complaining about problems, without ever getting down to trying to solve them.

It's important to spend at least as much time solving problems as complaining about them. Start by designating someone within your organization to track discussions at team meetings. Any problem that gets mentioned three or more times as an issue should be scheduled as an action agenda item at the next team meeting. You might also look back at all of the perennial problems in your organization. How many of them have you tried to solve in the past calendar year? And how many of them have you become comfortable just complaining about? Finally, make a simple rule that anyone who complains about a problem has to offer at least one suggestion for solving it.

■

Beware who walks through your open door

He pokes his head in the doorway and smiles, "Have you got a minute?"

I am very tempted to say, "No, I don't have a minute; I am busy until eternity." But I don't.

Instead, I say, "Come on in, Stan, and sit down and I will get you a cup of coffee." An hour later he leaves only because he has to go to the bathroom. Too much coffee, never enough talk.

My days can be an endless stream of people who line up outside my door and want just one minute of my time. They say that Abraham Lincoln in his first term of office would see anyone who came to his door. People would line up outside Lincoln's office to curry his favor, seek political appointments, or just talk. It doesn't sound like a great way to run a country. And it sure isn't an effective way to run a school district either.

As a modern school executive, you face a dilemma. You want to be accessible to people and be viewed as open and friendly. But you also need to get work done and follow some kind of a schedule. What do you do?

First, be sure your secretary knows how to screen people and can distinguish someone with an important issue that demands your immediate attention from someone who just wants to sit and gossip.

Second, devote a part of your weekly schedule to open office hours. Publish the times when you will be in your office and available to people. And then set a time limit on visits.

Most things in life, including informal meetings, can be accomplished in 15 minutes. This practice will let people know you are open for business to the public and let you operate in a less spontaneous environment. It will also help you deal with the people who come into your office and don't know how to find their way out again.

■

Choose (and plan) to be happy

I still vividly recall attending county superintendent meetings as a novice superintendent. Around the table sat 20 grizzled veterans. Each had countless war stories about their battles with parents, unions, and the Board. Their tales made it seem like everyone was a potential enemy except their immediate family and hunting dog. They seldom smiled and only talked passionately about retirement. After each meeting, I would promise myself that if I ever got that bad, I would do the world a favor and quit the profession.

I often wonder how school leaders get so cynical, negative, and pessimistic. Is it in the professional air we breathe or a natural scarring that happens over time with the many battles we fight?

Abraham Lincoln was right when he said "We can only be as happy as we will let ourselves be." We have to consciously rise above the negativity in our jobs and find a way to invigorate ourselves and renew the hope and optimism we had when we began our careers. Finding a way to stay happy should be a permanent professional goal, a goal that each of us can achieve in a different way.
Whenever I find myself becoming too sarcastic or

negative, I leave my office and spend time in class-rooms visiting kids. My favorite break is to visit our program for multiple-handicapped children. Every day these students have to overcome insurmountable obstacles, but somehow they manage to find a way to be happy. They help me place my life back into perspective and make me realize once again why I am in education.

You need to do the same thing. Find an activity or responsibility that brings out the best in you. And then be sure to consciously do it whenever the going gets tough.

■

Choose your words,
and use your power, carefully

R achel was known as a person of few words. Often she would attend meetings and say nothing until the end. Then she would clearly summarize an important issue, clarify an idea, or convincingly give her opinion. When she spoke, others knew what she said would be important and they listened carefully. By carefully choosing what to say and when to say it, she magnified the importance and impact of her comments.

The same can hold true for how you use power. By carefully picking when and where to use your power, you can increase your impact within an organization. Not all issues are worthy of your attention. If you become known as someone who gets involved in too many issues, you will dilute your influence and lose credibility. On the other hand, if you limit your involvement, you will send a clear message to others in the organization about what you believe is important.

■

Don't burn your bridges, especially while you're still standing on them

Joyce Brown was taking early retirement from her district. It was not an amicable parting. The composition of the Board had changed and become intensely political. Relationships had soured, and she had been given a choice between taking early retirement or being forced out of the district. She opted for a graceful exit—until her retirement party.

In her parting speech, Joyce was honest—way too honest. She readily admitted she was being fired. She singled out Board members for wanting to run the district and having private agendas. She chastised staff members for lacking courage and rolling over and playing dead.

As you can imagine, her speech was not well received. People sat in stunned silence. No one expected Joyce to say what they had all been thinking. Unfortunately, in the process of acting out a fantasy, she made herself permanently unemployable.

We all know that womb-to-tomb jobs in school districts are pretty much a thing of the past. How you handle yourself when leaving a difficult situation will speak volumes to a potential employer. Grace, dignity, humor, and some controlled honesty is helpful. Sometimes a simple "It just didn't work out" is enough. When speaking publicly, thank the people who deserve your gratitude and ignore the rest. And remember, if an act feels too good while you're doing it, it's probably illegal, or just a very bad idea.

Don't do other people's thinking

For the third time this week, Tom Fulton, the high school principal, is in my office telling me about a problem. This time it's a teacher who refuses to return her students' papers on time. As is usually the case, Tom ends his story with, "Now what should I do?"

Instead of curtly replying "get out of my office and solve your own problems," I ask, "What's your recommendation, Tom?"

"I don't know," he replies. "If I knew what to do, I wouldn't be here talking to you." Now I am getting irritated.

"Tom, until you decide what to do, you shouldn't be here. I am happy to react to your ideas, but you have to do more than just dump your problems at my door. I expect you to solve problems, not just report them."

Tom is confused. He thinks his role in the organization is to identify problems for someone else to solve. With his management style, he avoids responsibility and accountability. It's never his fault when things don't work out!

Avoid the pitfall of making decisions for other administrators. If you fall into this management pattern, you alone will be accountable. If you let that happen, get your resume ready, your days are numbered.

Don't forget to look in the closets

During my first week as a new superintendent the phone rang. It was a reporter from the largest newspaper in town.

"I am calling to confirm that you have a teacher on staff who has been charged with the sexual abuse of a minor. Our sources tell us this case has been ongoing for two years, and the teacher is about to return to your school from a leave of absence. Is this true? And, if so, why is your school district employing this kind of a person to work with children?"

Welcome to the delightful world of school administration!

I was at a total loss for an answer. Who was this person? No one had ever mentioned this bombshell to me in any interviews or prep meetings. I told the reporter I would have to verify my facts with staff and that I would call her back later in the day.

I immediately called my central office staff into a meeting.

"How many of you knew about this situation?" I asked.

Reluctantly, most of the people around the table sheepishly raised their hands. Several people looked at the floor, others shrugged their shoulders. Finally, someone said, "I didn't want to be the one who had to tell you."

Then someone else added, "We just didn't know how to bring it up in polite conversation."

While I wanted to blame everyone in my new district, I had to share the blame equally. Part of my ignorance was my own fault. I didn't ask enough questions. I should have asked, "Do you have any unusual or difficult personnel issues pending in the district?" I should have also stressed how much I hate surprises and that I expected people to warn me about impending doom before any bombs dropped.

Remember as you enter a new job to reserve a healthy sense of skepticism. And try to get introduced to at least some of the skeletons in your school district's closet before they fall out on you.

■

Don't let the urgent push out the important

It had been a fairly typical Board meeting. We reviewed the tentative budget for the coming school year, discussed at length minor changes in our employee health benefits program, and approved a school calendar guaranteed to accommodate the greatest number of vacation plans.

Toward the end of the meeting, a Board member spoke up with exasperation in her voice. "Our mission statement says that children are our highest priority, but we never seem to find the time to talk about them. Our meetings are filled with audits, textbook changes, and purchase orders. Are we ever going to get around to talking about kids?"

It was (and is) a good question. Why don't we spend our time on the things we say are important? We say we value kids, but rarely find the time to talk about key issues affecting them. We stress the importance of teaching, but spend more time in our office behind a desk than in a classroom observing teaching and learning. And we preach about the importance of the human touch in our organizations, but revert to memos and e-mail.

The most obvious display of what we believe is important in our schools is how we use our own time. As you review your monthly calendar, keep this in mind. And be sure to spend your time on the things you value.

■

20

Don't paint yourself into a professional corner

Fred was genuinely perplexed. He had been an assistant principal for the past six years. He was a perennial candidate for every new position listed in surrounding school districts.

"I don't understand it," he said. "I apply for positions and then I get interviewed and then I get rejected. Why doesn't anyone want to hire me? What am I doing wrong?"

"I don't think it's anything you've done wrong, Fred. I think it's what you haven't done right. What can you do today that you couldn't do six years ago? What skills do you have today that you didn't have six years ago?" I asked him.

Fred was a classic case of an "administrative wannabee"; someone who desperately wants to move forward in his career, but hasn't done what it takes to move to the next level of administration. As an assistant principal, he was responsible for student discipline and attendance. But the next job required a knowledge of curriculum, budgets, and staff evaluation. In narrowly following his job description, Fred had painted himself into a professional corner.

If you plan to advance in your career, you need to develop marketable skills. You need to research what skills will be needed at the next level and then develop a plan to get those skills. For instance, if a new position requires you to evaluate staff and you have no experience in your current position, volunteer to evaluate several teachers. If you need budget experience, consider assisting the budget office in preparing the annual budget. No one in schools ever turns down a volunteer.

You should constantly ask yourself career questions: What can I do today that I couldn't do last year? What is the most important skill for me to develop in the coming year? What is the one item I could add to my resume that would make me more competitive in the job market?

More coursework isn't the solution; it is a given. People expect you to have additional classes as part of your administrator's certification program or as part of earning an advanced degree. But everyone knows that coursework doesn't necessarily compute into marketable skills.

The only difference between a rut and a grave is depth. You need to continue to grow personally and professionally or get used to being where you are for the rest of your career.

■

Don't spend 45 minutes giving a 10-minute speech

As I listened to his speech drone on, I thought of Abraham Lincoln and Edward Everett at Gettysburg. Everett was the featured speaker; he talked for over two hours. His speech is now a forgotten footnote in history in comparison to Lincoln's masterpiece of brevity. Lincoln clearly summarized in 237 words the importance of the Civil War and the sacrifices of those who paid the ultimate price to preserve the Union. Two hours of talk versus 237 words packed with meaning and emotion.

After the speech reached its merciful conclusion, I approached the podium to introduce myself to the speaker.

"What did you think of my speech?" he asked.

"I thought you gave a great 10-minute speech," I replied.

"But my speech was 45-minutes long," he said with a puzzled look on his face.

"I know," I said. "I know."

Too many of us approach public speaking as if we are being judged by how much we have to say and not the quality of what gets said. But none of us gets paid by the word. Public speeches aren't contests to see how long we can talk. Rather, speeches should be approached from the opposite point of view—how long will your audience listen? With few exceptions, speeches should be prepared as if you were packing for a business trip: After you think you have finished packing, take out half of what is in your suitcase. You will still have enough to be suitably dressed. In the same fashion, write your speech and then seriously edit it to the bone. Your meaning and impact will be strengthened by what gets left out.

Remember that most audiences no longer have the patience to sit and listen for an hour. They have been conditioned by television and info-mercials. After 10 minutes, they will expect a commercial or a conclusion. Which one will you give them?

■

Don't try to bite off more than you can chew; you'll choke

L ike a lot of administrators, I am a compulsive list maker. I try to convince myself that if I make a list I won't forget quite so many things and my productivity will increase. At least that's how the theory goes.

Early in my career, I made a list every Monday morning of the things I needed to complete that week. Sometimes the list would be two pages long; by Tuesday afternoon, I had usually lost it underneath piles of paper on my desk.

25

A little later in my career, I decided I would simplify my life. Every morning I composed a daily list of what needed to be done. While the list was shorter, the results weren't much better. If I could find my list at the end of the day, I would be frustrated to see what didn't get done. All of the important items on my "hit list" got pushed aside by phone calls, brush fires, and everyone else's priorities.

So I have revised my daily battle plan one last time. Now I start each morning by listing the three most important jobs I have to finish. The list is short and doable and forces me to focus my time and energies on what is essential. As a result, I am a little less frustrated at the end of my work day. I no longer have to face a long list of things that never get done, and I usually finish the days feeling proud to have accomplished at least a few of my priorities.

■

Don't use a $1,000 meeting to solve a $10 problem

Next time you are in a seemingly endless meeting, do a little math. Multiply the number of people attending by their hourly pay. You will probably be shocked at the result.

Too often we have $1,000 meetings to solve $10 problems. Here are four simple rules for making meetings shorter and more productive:

(1) Never meet without an agenda or goal.

(2) Set time limits for every meeting and every item on your agenda.

(3) Organize your meeting so important issues get discussed first when people are wide awake, paying attention, and still capable of making good decisions.

(4) Set curfews. Never meet late into the night. Make a Board policy, if necessary, to adjourn all meetings by midnight. It's better to schedule another meeting at a later date than to make horrendous decisions in the early morning hours when tempers flare and emotion, not logic, prevails.

And never be afraid to cancel a meeting. I have yet to hear someone complain about the cancellation of an unnecessary meeting.

■

Even in the dry season there is water in the well, if only you lower your bucket

A few years ago I traveled to Africa and visited a village on the edge of the Kalahari Desert. For generation after generation, the people in the village had used the same well. Serious droughts were common in the region and water was a precious commodity. But in good times and bad, the people would go to the well and lower their buckets. They had a blind faith that there would always be water for them.

I asked one of the oldest men in the village, "Has there ever been a time when there was no water. What happens if the bucket is empty when you draw it up?"

"We believe there will be water," he replied.

I pressed on. "Yes, but what if there is no water?"

"Then life will go on. Somehow we survive," he said.

Much of his tribal life was based on such simple faith. There would be enough water, even in times of drought. Even in times of famine, there would be food. And when there was no water and no food, he had faith in the rest of the village that others would share.

It's a long way from Africa to Illinois, but I find more similarities than differences in the lives of the villagers in Africa and my own. So much of our personal and professional lives is governed by faith. The simple faith in our own ability to get the job done. The faith that our employer is honorable and will return our trust and loyalty. A faith that the people we work with each day will remain committed to the task at hand. And an unbending faith that what we do each day will make a difference in the lives of children. To lose our faith is to succumb to cynicism and to despair. To keep our faith is to keep the promise that lead us to become educators in the first place.

■

Get personal

As a principal several years ago, I decided to handwrite personal notes to all of the graduating seniors who had received awards in my high school. Halfway through the job, I changed my mind. Why should I write notes to only award winners? Wasn't every one of the students worthy of recognition and personal attention? Wouldn't it be a much better message to write a personal note to every graduating senior? So I set out to write a short message of thanks, congratulations, and encouragement to each of the seniors—no small task with a graduating class of 690.

All summer long there was a large stack of stationery on the corner of my desk. During phone calls and free moments, I wrote notes. At night while watching TV, I wrote more notes. Staff made fun of me. Was I writing notes in my sleep? Did I keep stationery in the bathroom? Was I going to send everyone in China a personal note, too?

By the end of the summer I had completed my goal. But I soon wondered whether the enormous effort was really worth it?

I got a very strong and positive answer to my question. Students and parents were surprised and pleased. No one was surprised that the valedictorian got a note, but they were very surprised when the students in the bottom of the class academically got theirs. Many students had never received a personal card or note from anyone while in high school. Students kept the cards and posted in places of honor, including on more than a few refrigerators across town.

In an era when you can easily generate hundreds of "customized" form letters by computer, why handwrite a note? Because no one expects you to do it. Because it says to the person who receives it: You are worth my time, you are important, and I care about you.

The larger the organization, the more important it becomes to keep the personal touch. Even on the busiest day, you need to find the time to personalize your approach to people and your job.

■

Head cheerleader needed!

L ots of people finish meetings by going around the table and asking staff for updates about their areas of responsibility. That's too predictable. So, instead, I occasionally ask people to tell me the best thing that has happened to them on the job during the week. I always get the same response. Panic!

Many of us don't know how to respond when we are asked to be positive. It's not in the job description. We can readily complain about our computers going down, or unproductive staff, or an unappreciative public. But when we are asked to be positive, we get downright squeamish: "Oh, no, next he will have us sitting on the floor in a circle singing Kumbiya."

What is it in human nature that makes being negative so much easier for some of us? Too many of us feel uncomfortable being "cheerleaders" for the organization? We believe that highlighting what is going right is a form of bragging we must avoid. We think we have more productive things to do with our time. We're dead wrong.

One of the most important things a leader does is set the tone and climate for the organization. Despite the negative tone around the water cooler, most people really want to feel good about where they work. They want to be successful and they want their organization to be successful, too.

People will rarely come to you with inspirational stories of success. They will more quickly come to you with problems and their thoughts about what is wrong in the organization. They view you as a problem-solver and the head of the company complaint department. The good news goes somewhere else.

I often remind myself about the formula in journalism that for every inch of negative press, you need 10 inches of positive press. The ratio may be even higher for public schools. To counter-balance the negative, you need to aggressively "sell" your schools. Your job description should have a line reading: Must function effectively as the chief cheerleader for the school.

And don't pay attention to what others say about your enthusiasm. You will be called worse things than Pollyanna in your career.

■

Help your colleagues go out with a bang rather than a whimper

Phil is a veteran teacher two years away from retirement. He is experiencing increasing problems with his students. Our evaluation conference is not going well. Phil is tired, frustrated, and wants out.

"Phil, I have in front of me a stack of referral slips to the main office for everything from sleeping to fighting. The number of complaints from the parents of your students is the highest in the school. And the failure rate of your students is double what it was two years ago. I know you are several years from retirement, but I need to see changes in your performance and work with students or I will have to place you on a program of remediation."

Phil only scowls back at me. My threat to implement a remediation plan bounces right off. He knows it takes at least three years and several hundred thousand dollars to dismiss a tenured teacher. Time and the system are on his side. I need to face reality, drop the threats, and implement a different plan.

I realize that instead of threats of punishment, Phil needs extra support and encouragement, maybe in the form of a change of scenery and working conditions. I consider proposing a number of ideas to Phil. I could have him mentor that enthusiastic new teacher in his department. I could offer to let him teach a new course, or co-chair the facilities study in his building. Clearly, I must give him a task where he can be successful, and expose him to positive, excited people. And, in the meantime, I will be sure that our best deans work with him on the discipline problems he is facing with his students.

We all need to finish our careers with our heads held high. Therefore, we must let veteran employees in the twilight of their careers know they still have value to the system. Instead of threatening people who cannot be threatened, we need to continue to work closely with them to ensure that their performances don't deteriorate and their careers don't end on a sour note. We must find a way to help them contribute until the end so they can go out with a bang instead of a whimper.

■

Hire people who have already made their share of mistakes

We are all out there desperately searching for the perfect employee. The person who graduated with honors from a prestigious Ivy League college, has published extensively, speaks flawless English, and has multiple Employee of the Year awards. In short, someone who doesn't exist.

So, instead, when looking for new employees, I search for the right "imperfect people." One of my favorite interview questions is "Tell me about the biggest mistake you have made this year and what you learned from it." Job candidates' responses tell me much about their truthfulness, learning curve, and potential for growth.

People who have made their share of mistakes in past jobs are at an advantage. Making mistakes is a by-product, and occasional consequence, of taking action. Chances are people who don't make mistakes, don't make very many decisions. People who openly acknowledge and learn from their mistakes usually know how to accept and put into perspective their own failures and the failures of others. They have learned how to face failure, persevere, and move forward with their lives. They are a little more tolerant of the frailties of others and a little less likely to judge harshly the shortcomings of their colleagues.

Remember, there is a huge difference between people who have failed and failures.

■

If we all think alike, are we all necessary?

We had just completed a national search for a new assistant superintendent for business. After interviewing 10 candidates, we had a finalist. I felt very comfortable with the person; we had mutual interests, skills, and personalities. We were very much alike, in fact, too alike. A small warning bell began ringing loudly in the back of my head. It was signaling I was about to make a classic mistake. I was about to hire myself.

As you build a management team, you need to valiantly fight the impulse to hire people who walk like you, talk like you, and think like you. Not everyone needs to agree with all of your personal beliefs as a condition of employment. Even though it can be uncomfortable, dissent is healthy. A balanced team needs members who will argue politely, disagree respectfully, and challenge ideas that need to be questioned.

If you take a plan for changing the administrative structure of your organization to your team and everyone automatically agrees with it, will the final plan be as strong as if teams members aggressively challenge your ideas and make you defend and explain your plan in detail?

Team members are valuable to the extent they can contribute, critique, and improve plans, rather than how often they can shake their heads "Yes" and make you feel important. Try to consciously hire a diverse team of people from different backgrounds and with different life experiences who can bring something unique to the table. In the end, the success of your team will be directly related to the number of free and creative thinkers you have around the table.

■

If you can't write it on your tombstone, it's probably not important

It was impossible for me to believe I was standing in a cemetery helping bury one of my favorite students on such a quite, lovely summer morning.

Dan Lutz wasn't just another student, he was exceptional—bright, witty, athletic, the kind of kid who teenagers and adults loved. In less than one year, Dan had gone from the top of his class and a scholarship at an Ivy League school to committing suicide. What could have happened? It was inconceivable to us that he could have killed himself. Why would he have done such a thing?

When his final grade report arrived from the East coast, we knew. Dan had failed a class and been placed on academic probation. Dan had never failed anything in his life. We had all amply prepared him for success, but he was simply unable to handle failure.

When the graveside service ended, Dan's mother and I lingered by his tombstone, not ready to leave, not knowing what to say. She broke the silence.

37

"It doesn't matter anymore whether his room was dirty or that he played his music too loud, or had friends I didn't like. None of it matters; it wasn't important then and it isn't important now."

I reached over and put my arm around her. We looked down at his tombstone. On it was written simply:

Dan Lutz
Beloved Son and Brother
1970-1988

Dan's death has caused me to continually reassess what is important in my own life and to put my own successes and failures in their proper light. In one way or another, we all face the danger of losing perspective. We take insignificant issues in our jobs and our lives much too seriously. We lose track of what is really important.

Take a moment right now. Reach into your desk drawer and get a 3 X 5 card. Write your own epitaph on the card. As people stand in a distant cemetery years from now, what will they read when they look down at your tombstone? How will you summarize who you were and what you stood for in your life? What's important to you?

■

Ignored problems seldom solve themselves

Mr. Jordan was my high school U.S. history teacher. He was a chronic alcoholic who slept through more classes than his students, so most of his students eventually cut an informal deal with him—we'll leave you alone, if you leave us alone. Generations of students in my town took his class, kept their mouths shut, and enjoyed the extra study hall. We could never quite understand, though, why Mr. Jordan wasn't fired. Wasn't being drunk on the job against the rules? Thirty years later, I have figured it out.

The administration at my school knew Mr. Jordan had a drinking problem. They cut the same informal deal with him that his students had. They consciously chose to ignore the problem. They probably had plenty of excuses: "It's impossible to fire a tenured teacher." "He only has two more years to go until retirement." "It would take too much time and cost too much money to get rid of him." "He isn't really hurting anyone but himself." "It would be too hard to prove and, after all, we're school administrators not cops."

Each of us can manufacture loads of excuses for not doing our jobs. The more difficult the problem, the easier it is to create excuses. But ignoring problems, minimizing them, or pretending they don't exist won't make them go away. And unattended, most problems only fester and grow uglier.

■

It's all about
relationships—All of it

My father was in management in the automotive industry. I remember him going out evenings to visit employees in the hospital or to attend wakes, funerals, and weddings. I could never understand why.

One day I asked, "Dad, why do you spend so much time visiting people I haven't ever met?"

He replied, "It's an important part of my job. Being a boss is like being the head of a large family. You have to show people that you care about them and that they are important."

Recently, one of our high school students had a life-threatening illness. I took a Friday afternoon off to visit her in the hospital. The following week, several people in the community told me how impressed they were that a superintendent would take time to visit a sick student.

Never forget you are the official representative of your district. Not only do you set the budget, you also set the moral tone. You are the most important role model in the district. People might not understand what your job entails, but they do know something about what it takes to be a decent human being. Show them that you know too.

■

Keep an open mind;
you might learn something

It's a late Friday afternoon, and I am sitting at my desk writing thank you notes. I picked up the habit 20 years ago because of Charlie Fredericks. Charlie was a high school principal, and I was a young, highly opinionated department chair. We frequently argued over student placements and discipline decisions.

One memorable time, Charlie and I fought over a student who was creating problems in and out of school. I thought she deserved to be expelled; Charlie thought she deserved more attention. He went on and on about the girl's alcoholic father and abusive mother. How could any 17-year-old girl succeed or even survive with the odds she faced each day? He argued that we needed to be her surrogate family. If we did nothing for her and she dropped out of school, what had we proved? I told him his bleeding heart was ruining my carpet.

Charlie eventually got his way; the organizational chart was on his side. The young girl was placed back in all of her classes. The year passed and the girl, with time and Charlie's personal attention, developed into an above-average student. In the spring, she graduated and was accepted at a local college.

The day after graduation, I sat down and wrote Charlie a personal note. I sincerely thanked him for making a great decision. I admitted he was right and I had been wrong. I encouraged him to continue to champion the kids who everyone else gave up on. I told him we were a better school because we had a caring leader at the helm.

The next morning Charlie appeared in my doorway with my letter in his hand and tears in his eyes. My note had touched him and he didn't know what to say. For the next few years, we continued to fight, but our friendship deepened. Then I took another position and Charlie stayed on.

A decade passed and I decided to take a nostalgic trip back to where I started out as an administrator. Charlie was still principal, championing the cause of troubled kids. I sat in his office and wondered how many students had sat in the same chair and felt good because they knew that the guy in charge cared about them.

While we reminisced, I looked around his office at 30 years of collected mementos. In a far corner, I saw a framed letter displayed on the wall. It was my thank you letter.

"Charlie, I can't believe it. You kept my letter and framed it. I am really touched"

"Don't be. It's a visible reminder to me that I was always right and you were always wrong," he laughed.

Because of Charlie's influence, I promised myself a long time ago that I'd spend Friday afternoons writing personal notes to teachers, parents, students, and other colleagues. It was a great decision. It makes me and other people feel good, and it's a great way to end any work week.

■

Know when to laugh—
at yourself and with others

It seemed like such a simple idea—a charity basketball game in the local high school gym featuring a team of teachers and notable personalities from town. Not much planning was necessary, there would be few overhead expenses, and the proceeds could go to a local charity. What could possibly go wrong?

The gym was packed the night of the big game with almost every family in town. The band was playing and everything was going smoothly until midway into the second quarter when two young men wearing only gym shoes and ski masks ran across the gym floor and out the backdoor into a waiting car. Some of the parents were horrified. They surely hadn't expected to have their young children exposed to full frontal nudity at a school-sponsored event. Who was in charge? Someone had to be punished and it probably wasn't going to be the two guys in the ski masks.

I appeared the following week at the Board meeting to experience firsthand the outrage of the town citizenry and the wrath of the school board. I was eventually called upon to explain my role in the unsavory episode. I told the Board in detail about planning for the event and the security measures we had taken.

"How could you let such a spectacle occur in our building?" an outraged Board member asked. There was a chorus of amens from the audience.

"I don't mean to make light of the situation and its seriousness, but if someone is bent on taking off his clothes and running naked in the world there isn't much I can do to prevent it from happening," I responded. "I don't know of any insurance policy we could purchase that would protect us from bare-naked people. I guess we could form a Board committee and interview all of the male students one-by-one to see if they were involved. Of course, this might not be a real good idea because they would all have to be naked so we could make a positive i.d."

I hoped humor would ease some of the tension and put the incident in its true perspective.

Halfway through my comments, I could see Board members beginning to smile. Several of them stifled chuckles as they tried to visualize themselves interviewing 500 naked young men in the gym. I was let off with a gentle reprimand and no record of the incident was ever placed in my personnel file.

Sometimes the worst thing you can do is to treat a situation too seriously. Humor, when used appropriately, can diffuse angry crowds and ugly situations. So learn to laugh at yourself, at life, and with others.

■

Leadership is situational

Barbara Reese had been a highly successful administrator in three other school districts. But after six months on the new job, Barbara was on the ropes.

"Dennis, I don't know what is going wrong," she said. "I'm doing exactly the same things that have worked so well in other schools. Yet, every time I turn around a bomb is going off in my face. What should I do?"

Barbara failed to understand that leadership is highly situational. What works in one school may not work in another.

Leading an organization is like raising children. Most children are basically the same. They all have the same basic needs and desires. But it's the details that drive parents mad. Just when you think you have your parenting skills finely honed with one child, another comes along and nothing seems to work. You practically have to learn how to be a parent all over again.

The same is true with schools. They are all basically alike, but it's the subtle differences that can drive you crazy. Like people, schools have different personalities, priorities, and goals. Sports programs might be the tail that wags the dog in one school and another might only emphasize academics. In one school, the teachers union might be friendly, and in another it might be a leader's arch enemy. There are schools where the building leader is a demi-god and others where the "leader" is nothing but a powerless figurehead.

When you change jobs you will have to change more than your address and phone number; you might also have to change your management style and how you relate to and communicate with people. So when you get ready to change jobs, seriously survey the new landscape and assess what kind of changes you will need to make in how you operate.

■

Leadership lessons around the kitchen table

It's 1958 and I am sitting at the kitchen table with my parents and my seven brothers and sisters. I sit in the middle of the table where the mashed potatoes converge with the roast beef and peas. I don't realize it, but every night I'm getting a basic course in Leadership 101.

Our family runs as a modified democracy. My father cares what we think and wants us to learn how to make decisions, but when a final decision needs to be made, we know who is in charge and who is ultimately responsible.

We clearly understand the organizational chart. My father and mother are at the top and we are at the bottom. Each of us has a role and responsibility in the family. As a 10-year-old, my role is to listen attentively to everything adults say; I'm responsible for setting the table for dinner and shutting up unless spoken to.

Communication is clear and direct. Over and over again, we hear about the importance of teamwork and getting the job done. Is our homework finished? Did we do our chores? What happened in school today? This isn't idle chit-chat, but a continual reinforcement of our family's values and beliefs.

Frequently, stories are told about family history and favorite and infamous relatives. My father's stories tell us who we are, what we believe, and what we need to support as a family.

I learned more about leadership at the kitchen table than in any graduate course I have taken as an adult. Important messages about communicating effectively, being responsible and loyal to others, and the importance of teamwork and storytelling.

What did you learn? Think back to your own family dinner table. What lessons did you learn that could help you today, besides the importance of passing food clockwise around the table?

Leaders, like great chefs, know when to alter the recipe

I knew a high school principal who hid behind the rules. Every decision sent him scurrying to the policy manual or student handbook. His personal Waterloo was a 16-year-old girl with a paring knife.

An appeal came to my office on a 10-day suspension. The case involved a girl who was charged with possessing a weapon, a paring knife, in school. I called the principal into my office for more details on the case.

"It's a clear-cut case," he said. "She violated the student handbook. It clearly states, no knives in school."

"Could you give me a few of the details, Don? Where did it happen, what time of day, and who was involved?" I asked.

As the story unfolded, I became more and more upset.

The girl came to school early every morning. Often she would quietly sit in an empty hallway and eat her breakfast. On the morning of the incident, she was by herself eating an apple. Because she wore braces and peelings from apples stuck in them, she was peeling the apple before eating it. As a teacher walked by, she saw the girl with a paring knife in her hand. She immediately reported her to the principal's office.

"Don," I said, "How can we suspend a girl for 10 days for cutting up an apple?"

He replied, "But we have given that punishment to every other student who brought a weapon to school. Why should she be any different?"

"You get paid to make decisions based on common sense, Don. The girl might have exercised bad judgment by bringing a paring knife to school, but this was not a weapon anymore than carrying a baseball bat down the hallway to baseball practice is."

After we talked through the case at length, Don decided it would be better to simply discuss the problem with the girl and send her home for the day.

Too many people act as "cookbook" leaders. These people wrongly believe that you can create a policy or procedure for everything that can conceivably happen in a district and that, like when baking a cake, all they need to do is follow the recipe. But true leadership demands something more than a cookbook. It requires creativity, imagination, and fairness.

49

■

Leaders pick up paper in the parking lot

I was standing by the backdoor of the school building waiting for a finalist for our high school principal job to arrive. Across the parking lot, I could see him get out of his car and slowly begin to walk across the lot. He took his time, carefully checking out our property, and stopping occasionally to pick up paper. When he came to the end of the parking lot, he threw the paper he had picked up in a trash can. I greeted him as he entered the building. After we introduced each other and passed pleasantries, I told him I had been watching him.

"Why did you pick up the garbage in the parking lot?" I asked.

"If I walk past trash in a school parking lot and don't pick it up, what am I saying to students and staff and you?" he asked me.

Great answer I thought.

We eventually hired him. I figured that if as a stranger he picked up trash in our parking lot, as an employee he would do even more. I was right. John Young turned out to be the best high school principal I have ever known. Every day he models what he believes. And it goes far beyond picking up paper. He helps set the tone in a school where people are responsible for themselves and for each other; where staff and students are less likely to throw paper on the ground and much more likely to think it is their responsibility to pick it up.

■

Listen to yourself speak

Do you keep a speech file? I do. It can be very helpful to reread past speeches. They should be the public record of what we value and believe. There should be a constant theme and moral to what we say in public. And there should be a direct relationship between what we say in public and the actions we take everyday.

It is perfectly acceptable, even preferable, to repeat the same idea in speeches. There are surprisingly few themes we need to continually emphasize—the importance of a good basic education, the inherent value of every child, the role we all have in supporting education. We have so few real opportunities to promote our message that we need to be clear, consistent, and focused. Repeating the same message can be helpful. Your audience can learn through repetition, and so can you.

It's also a good idea to get in the habit of listening to your own "sermons." About twice a year, sit down and go through speeches you have given over the past few years. The time spent is always valuable. It will help you remember what you have publicly "promised" people and should help refocus your attention on what is important.

51

Long after people have forgotten your name, they will remember how you treated them

As I move toward the end of my career, I become more reflective and think more about the influence I have had on others. How will people remember me when I am gone? Did I make a difference in the lives of others? Was it all worthwhile?

Last month I received a letter from a parent. Her son had graduated from high school when I was a principal in the early 1980s. Lots of time had passed and she had a difficult time locating me, but she wanted to tell me what had happened to her son.

I had wondered on occasion what had happened to Tim. He was a memorable student, but for all the wrong reasons. In high school, Tim was immature, with a volatile temper and absolutely no motivation. He was frequently in my office for a laundry list of misbehaviors. Tim was always on the brink—one step from dropping out and one step from being expelled.

I remember a key meeting I had with him in late fall of his senior year. Tim's father had just died after a long fight against cancer. The ordeal had left its mark on the family, and especially on Tim.

What was the point in school? No one cared, and those did died.

Tim needed to talk about his father and his life. He desperately needed a place to cry and for someone to quietly listen. We spent the afternoon going through a box of tissues. I heard about family fishing trips, Tim and his father rebuilding cars, and Tim's fears that he could never feel close to someone again in his life. At the end of the afternoon, Tim decided that he would try to finish school. It was going to be his way of honoring his father.

Tim graduated and moved out of my life. His mother's letter was a belated thank you. Tim had gone through a stint in the military and then on to college. He was just finishing graduate school and had been promoted in his jobs, and he and his wife were expecting their first child. His mother wanted me to know she had not forgotten what I had done for her son.

You see, to be a leader you need to do more than make good decisions. You need to have the wisdom to intervene at key times in peoples' lives to give them the support and understanding they need to put their lives back together and to become whole. Whether it's a 15-year-old student struggling through school, a 45-year-old math teacher who has temporarily lost his motivation to teach, or a 64-year-old secretary who is ill but wants to work just one more year, they will all need something from you. More often than not, it will be something so simple you might dismiss it—a kind word, a gentle hand on a tired shoulder, or a smile at the end of a long difficult day.

Isn't it remarkable how simple but amazingly complex our jobs and lives can be?

Make it easy for people to tell you bad news

As you climb the organizational ladder, you will be surprised what employees will and won't tell you. They will openly share with you their successes along with the failures of others. But it's a rare person who will share his own failure with you or give you insights into a failure within the system. Most people simply don't want to be associated with bad news, particularly if it reflects back on them.

Expecting people to report their own mistakes isn't reasonable. Expecting them to report the mistakes of their colleagues is just as bad. It doesn't work in prisons or schools. No one likes or trusts a snitch.

If you want to get an accurate idea of the problems in your school, talk to people who have nothing to gain or lose from being brutally honest. Here are three sources of reliable, accurate information:

* Conduct exit interviews with retiring employees. Ask them about the programs they have worked in and what problems need to be addressed. Ask them for solutions. Retirees often know how to solve long-standing problems, but are never asked for their opinions. Exit interviews can be a formal way of recognizing retirees' contributions and saying thank you for their service.

* Interview students and families leaving your school or district. Quite often these families have been in multiple schools and have been exposed to different types of programs. They will freely share their opinions about the best and weakest teachers, as well as other useful information.

* Survey graduating seniors about a year after they leave school. They will let you know in clear terms what worked and what didn't. They should also be in a position to let you know how well they were prepared for college or a career.

■

Make yourself necessary to somebody

She was obviously lost, walking down a long, empty hallway, pausing in front of doors and checking a slip of paper in her hand.

"You look lost, can I help you?" I asked.

"I need to enroll my son," she said. "Where is the main office?"

"This is a big building and you could easily spend the rest of the day wandering the hallways. I know the way, let me walk you there."

As we walked down the hallway, we began a conversation and friendship that would span a decade and the high school education of her three children.

On another day I might have walked by with my head down and said nothing. Or I might have given her simple directions and gone on my way. Instead I chose to spend five minutes of my day helping someone. It wasn't part of my job description. I would never be evaluated on helping lost people find their way. Or would I?

I've had numerous other occasions in my career when I stopped to do a small favor for someone and it ultimately paid big dividends. Most of these encounters are spontaneous, unrehearsed, and seldom reappear. It may be quickly solving a problem on the phone instead of transferring it to someone else or showing someone courtesy and respect they won't receive anywhere else. It may be listening to a complaint and showing sympathy and compassion. If you can solve someone's problem quickly and effectively—do it. Like Ralph Waldo Emerson advised: "Make yourself necessary to somebody."

■

Most of the important things in life can be written on the back of your business card

L ike most people I know, I carry a small number of business cards in my wallet. I rarely pass them out as part of business, though. Instead, they serve as a constant reminder for me to keep the essentials in my life and career as simple as possible. I challenge myself to write down messages, ideas, and goals in the small space on the back of my business card. I also challenge my colleagues and friends to do the same. Often when people are trying to explain an idea to me I hand them one of my cards.

"Here, write down what you mean on this card," I say.

"You have to be kidding me," they usually respond. "I can't fit it all in that space."

"Sure you can, just be concise. You've got at least 50 words. Lincoln could have done the outline for the Gettysburg Address in that space, I'm sure you can make your idea fit, too."

This is the ultimate executive summary. There isn't room for educational jargon, fancy phrases, or extended metaphors. Try it for a while. It reinforces clear and direct communication. Either you and your colleagues will learn to be concise, succinct, and to the point, or you will learn how to write extremely small.

■

Most organizations and communities are led by less than 2% of their people

One year into my first superintendency, I would often get a feeling of déjà vu. It was like the episode in "The Twilight Zone" where you keep seeing the same people over and over again. It didn't matter where I was in the community. Whether I was at a Board meeting, a civic event, or a community fundraiser, the same people were waiting for me. My experience wasn't supernatural, though, it was reality. I was seeing the same people over and over again.

Most communities and organizations are lead by a surprisingly small number of people. This is a blessed curse. It is a blessing because you only need to rally a small group of people to get a new idea or program started. It is a curse because without the support of this small group your next proposal or initiative can be dead on arrival.

One of your first jobs as a leader is to quickly learn where the power lies and who are the power brokers. This group is the backbone of your communications network. You have to be certain they clearly understand the goals and directions of your organization. If they don't understand your message, no one will. So, before you proceed with any major project, you must anticipate how these individuals will react to the project and bring them along. With them in your corner, your life will be much easier—and you will be much more successful at getting the right things done.

■

Never confuse the number of hours you work with your value to the organization

Any time two or more administrators get together and talk shop, they naturally gravitate to two subjects: who has the worst Board, and who works the most 14-hour days. It's shocking how many of us publicly boast about the crazy hours we work. We work on weekends, neglect our families, and refuse to take vacations. We think we are irreplaceable. But people who think they are indispensable die just like everyone else, though usually a little sooner.

You eventually reach a point of diminishing returns with 80-hour work weeks and begin to lose energy, drive, and interest. Some administrators work themselves into an emotional and physical wreck. If you are working too many endless weeks, you need to ask a few questions. Is all of the work I am trying to do really necessary? Is it my work, or am I covering for an incompetent subordinate? Do I know how to delegate? Have I set realistic goals? Do I have priorities, or has everything become equally important in my eyes?

Just remember when you say you are too busy to take a vacation, that's when you need one the most.

■

Never date the boss

He was desperate for a job. Very desperate. He decided to forego completing an application for the job and go directly to the source, the President of the Board of Education. She was a reasonably attractive woman. He called her office to inquire about a job listing. Later in the week, he took her to lunch. Later in the month, he began to date her.

Their courtship paralleled the hiring process. Their romance peaked the same month he was named as the new elementary school principal. Three months later, he unceremoniously dumped her. One month later, on a 4-3 vote, he was fired. The President of the Board cast the deciding vote. The last time I saw him, he was sitting in the corner of a hotel lobby at a state conference holding his head in his hands listening to an attorney read him his severance contract.

Romance often occurs in the workplace, but seldom works out. Basing one's career on an emotionally charged romantic relationship just isn't good business. If you want to get ahead professionally, set goals and work hard. If you are lonely, try a dating service.

■

Never mistake silence for consent

J ack was the superintendent of a large, rural district in the Midwest. He had been with the district for 15 years and was respected and admired by the community. His district desperately needed to pass a $20,000,000 referendum to complete renovations on two buildings and put a major addition on the high school. Plans were developed, public meetings were held, newsletters were sent out. Everything proceeded as planned. No organized opposition appeared. Everyone was optimistic the referendum would pass.

The day before the big vote, I spoke with Jack on the phone.

"What do you think about the vote? Will your referendum pass?" I asked.

Jack said, "I feel real good about it. No one has come out of the woodwork at us. We are pretty confident of success."

Two days later the headline in the local paper read: "School Referendum Goes Down in Flames."

How could a veteran leader and his staff so badly misread a community? Unfortunately, Jack made a common mistake. He mistook silence for consent. We get so used to people screaming their opinions at us that we don't know how to interpret silence. Just because no one is complaining doesn't mean there aren't problems in your district. Sometimes people don't know how to tell you the bad news. Instead of confronting you, they will avoid you and silently go into a voting booth and pull the NO lever.

This is why it's critical that you cultivate a small group of people—parents, staff and community members—who you can count on to tell you the truth no matter how ugly. You need people who have credibility and common sense, and who can tell the difference between fact and juicy gossip. Often these are people who don't rely on you for job security and who can hurt your feelings and survive. Seek out these people and make them part of your team.

And be just a little suspicious when things get too quiet in your district.

■

One of the keys of leadership is know-
ing when and how to tell people
things they don't want to hear

I n ancient Greece, the bearer of bad tidings was put to death.
Many of us remember this history lesson when it comes time to
share bad news.

Here is a strategy for sharing bad news. Be honest. Tell your Board
right up front that there will come a time when you will have to tell
them something they don't want to hear. It might be firing a popular but unproductive employee, or an emergency budget deficit, or
simply having to present a program they might not want to support. Always let them know about the problem in private and, if at
all possible, in advance of a Board meeting. Let them know you
will try never to surprise them in public and that you will always
give them the opportunity to talk you out of an unpopular idea or,
at least, to help you modify your plans before they become final.

Setting the groundwork for communicating bad news in advance
helps ease the pain. It lets the Board know that conflict is inevitable
and it's acceptable to disagree with one another if done in a professional, sensible manner. It also decreases the likelihood of you
repeating the fate of the Ancient Greek messenger.

63

■

One single person can be the difference in the lives of children

A few summers ago I traveled with my family on vacation to Northern Michigan. The highlight of our vacation was viewing one of the most spectacular meteorite showers in history. We spent an entire evening sitting on the shore of Lake Huron watching the night sky. For hours we sat in wonder watching the streaking flashes of light. It was an awe-inspiring display of nature.

The following morning at breakfast, my children could only talk about what they had witnessed the night before. I was curious about how much they really understood about what they'd seen.

"How big do you think one of those meteorites is that we saw last night?" I asked.

"As big as the moon," one of my daughters guessed.

"No, even bigger. As big as the sun," another argued.

"No, about as big as an asteroid," the oldest said with a knowing tone in her voice.

"None of you is even close," I said. "They were about as big as the grains of sand on the shore you were sitting on last night," I said.

They all laughed. Just another wild story from their father leading to some kind of an obscure lesson he was no doubt going to try to teach them.

It wasn't until I read them an article on meteorites from a national science journal later in the week that they would reluctantly believe me. It seemed impossible. Tiny grains of sand streaking through space and lighting up our sky. How could something so small create so much light? How could something as small as a grain of sand have such an impact in our universe?

It's amazing, but true. Given the right conditions, something the size of a grain of sand can light up a nighttime sky. And one single person with courage in the right place can have a profound impact on an organization. You could be that person who will literally light up the sky in your organization and shed light on every child if you have the courage and wisdom to act at the right time. Through dedication and perseverance, you, one single person, can make a difference.

65

Only Ma Bell profits from a phone call that lasts longer than 10 minutes

Have you ever had a day when you seemed tied to your phone? Your desk is littered with those little blue slips of paper that say, "While you were out." Nothing gets done and you go home with a funny, little, red circle on your ear and a kink in your neck from tilting your head sideways to hold the receiver against your shoulder. Here are a few hints that should make you more productive and cut in half the amount of time you waste on the phone.

First, keep a written record of every phone call you make or receive. This creates a paper trail for documenting at a later date what really got said in a conversation as opposed to what someone thought they remembered you saying.

Second, before you start each conversation, write down how long you expect the phone call to last.

Third, let the other person know about how much time you have to talk as you start the conversation. This won't insult people, but rather underscores that you are a busy person and have things to do.

And, lastly, when you have approached your time estimate, do a quick reality check. Have you completed what you needed to say? Does the other person need just a little more time to vent? Will more time be well spent or will you cover the same territory? Balance being respectful against getting your work done. If the purpose of the call has been completed, it's time to politely excuse yourself and go on to your next task.

■

Pick your battles wisely

Conflict is inherent between school leaders and school board members. Both want to run the same school system, and both possess many of the same personal characteristics. School leaders and board members are strong-willed, high-powered people who are used to getting their own way and making their own decisions. And often they are lousy team members.

Problems will surely arise if you forget who is the boss and who is the employee. Your ability to survive is directly related to your ability to stand firm on key issues and know when to compromise and negotiate on others. Having convictions isn't just being stubborn. Sometimes, as a matter of conscience, you have to face certain defeat; at other times, you can modify your position and still sleep at night. Your ability to make the right call can mean the difference between being fired and earning the admiration of your board.

Try to remember that you were hired to solve problems cooperatively with your Board, not to stand alone against it. Even the highest paid corporate CEO has to follow a board of directors. You might be an organizational whiz or an instructional wonder or both, but get on the wrong side of the majority of your board members, and your days are numbered. So pick your battles carefully, and try to avoid fighting with people who legally have the last word.

■

Pigs get fat; hogs get butchered

Jim Johnson had just accepted a new position as superintendent. He was ready to negotiate his contract and was getting lots of free advice.

"Get everything up front," some friends told him. "If you don't get it in your first contract, you will never get it."

Others said: "Ask for the moon and then settle for a little less. Be aggressive. They obviously want to hire you and will pay extra. You have them over a barrel. Take advantage of your position."

Jim decided to follow their advice. He demanded a higher salary than the retiring superintendent and a more comprehensive benefits package. He dug his heels in and stubbornly refused to budge.

Board members were taken aback by his aggressive stance. Several began to wonder if they had made a mistake.

The contract negotiations dragged on. When his contract was finally approved, it was on a 4-3 vote. Jim began his new job with three board members resentful and angry. At the first board election the following year, there was a shift of one seat. In the following year, he was dismissed on a 4-3 vote.

Creating an adversarial relationship with your employer, as you start a new job, is never a good idea. You need to promote and protect your career, but not at the expense of losing the support of the people who sign your paycheck. There is a big difference between protecting your interests and being seen as greedy. Instead of arguing with your future employer, try this approach.

First, never apply for a position that offers a starting salary less than you would accept. Trying to get a Board of Education to give you more money than they list in their job opening is very risky business. It is acceptable, however, to push for the top of the salary range.

Second, never use threats or emotion when arguing money. Use facts. Give the Board data on comparable area salaries with adjustments for your years of experience and degrees earned.

Third, if you can't get movement on your base salary, concentrate on other economic perks, like health benefits, life insurance, vacation days, and an annuity.

And, finally, if all else fails, hold your breath and be patient. If you want more money, work hard, do a good job, and then ask to re-negotiate your contract after the first year or two when you have shown the Board what you are really worth.

■

Promote employees for
the right reasons

Most people believed Alan Power was the best history teacher in the school district. He was a caring, humane person who motivated students to their maximum. Students flocked to his classes, and parents tried to pull strings to get their children into his class. Everyone loved Mr. Powers.

When an assistant principal's position in the district became vacant, Alan applied. The interview committee unanimously picked him for the job.

He began the school year with hopes of becoming the best administrator in the district. Six months later, he was in my office in tears.

"On most days I don't know whether I'm going to throw up, have a nervous breakdown, or quit," he groaned. "I don't know if I could even recognize a good student anymore. All I see are the dredges of society. If the kids aren't driving me crazy, their parents are. Everything is a problem and a big problem. What am I going to do?" he pleaded.

I squirmed in my seat and told him the truth.

"Alan, I think you need to tough it out for the rest of the school year and then request to return to the classroom where you really belong. You are a great teacher, but you're no longer teaching."

Alan was promoted because he was an exceptional teacher. Unfortunately, there is no direct relationship between being a great teacher and being a competent assistant principal. Lots of good people get promoted in schools for the wrong reasons. Great teachers are promoted out of their classrooms for their teaching talents, assistant principals are chosen as principals because they are tough disciplinarians, and ex-football coaches are named superintendent because they are highly visible and respected in their communities. None of these are examples, however, of good hiring practice. People should be promoted for what they can become not for what they have been. It's only fair to them—and everyone else.

■

Remember the gifts you have been given in life

Another graduation is approaching. I can't help but think back to all of the wonderful moments over the past 20 years. In particular, I remember the year Andy Adamson graduated.

Andy was one of the most remarkable young men I have ever met. He transferred into my school at the beginning of his junior year. By the time he made his way to the admissions office, he had made five new friends. Within a year, he was the president of his class, a captain of the football team, homecoming king, and the most popular boy in the school. He was also diagnosed with cancer. A minor leg injury in football had not healed, and then for no reason a bone in his right leg shattered. X-rays revealed a rare, aggressive form of bone cancer. The prognosis was pretty dismal.

Throughout his senior year, Andy went through extensive chemotherapy and radiation sessions. In the spring, his right leg was amputated. No one expected Andy to survive; no one ever expected him to return to school. Yet two weeks before graduation he was racing down the hallways on his crutches, planning his summer vacation and going to college in the fall. He was chosen by his classmates as one of two speakers at graduation.

Andy presented a striking contrast on stage in his cap and gown. He was a handsome, vibrant, young man but leaning on crutches with only one leg under his gown. His speech was memorable. The only reference to his illness was that it was a "misdiagnosed blessing." Instead of dwelling on his illness, he spoke about the gifts we are given in life and the responsibility we have to use those gifts for others. He talked about the gifts of friendship, love, and family.

There was no self-pity, anger, or resentment in his speech, only hope, kindness, and love. At the end of his speech, he asked each of the graduating seniors to make a list of the gifts they had been given in their lives and to carry the list with them as a permanent reminder of what was important in their lives. It was a heart-warming, touching message. We all smiled through our tears.

Six months after he graduated from high school, we buried Andy.

Last year I attended the 10-year reunion for his class. Early in the evening the conversation turned to Andy. At first people seemed reluctant to talk about him. After 10 years, you could still see pain in some of the students' eyes. Eventually though the stories became more animated and laughter replaced the tears.

One young man finally asked, "Do you remember what Andy said at graduation about making a list of the gifts we had been given in life?" They all nodded yes.

From a wallet or purse, each one of his friends produced a list of their "gifts in life." Written on the top of each sheet of paper was the name Andy Adamson.

■

Remember why you got the job
in the first place

You submitted your application for the job along with 75 other candidates. You were one of the five people they interviewed for the position. And then they selected you. After the initial euphoria and congratulatory phone calls, you begin to ask yourself questions. "Why did they hire me?" "What made me a better candidate than anyone else?" "What do I have that sets me apart from all of the others?"

An important part of setting your goals for the first year on a new job is finding out the answers to these questions. Over a lengthy career, I have had numerous people call me to find out why they weren't chosen for a position. But no one ever asks why they were successful. It's ironic that the only time we want to know how we are doing is when people reject us. Why not be different and go directly to the source and ask the people who interviewed and hired you why you were chosen?

In the first 30 days after getting a new job, make individual calls to the people who were instrumental in hiring you. Thank them for making such an intelligent decision. Then ask them a few pointed questions such as "What was the one thing that made you want to hire me?" "What were some of my past achievements that impressed you?" "What would you like to see me achieve in my first year on the new job?"

Compile your notes; type them in capital, bold-faced letters; and then laminate the sheets and post them in a spot where you will see them every work day. This is your "success formula" for your first year on the job.

■

Respect the opposition

A friend of mine was superintendent in a small town in Wisconsin. His board meetings were pleasant, orderly evenings with few surprises until an elderly gentleman began attending. This gentleman had lots of questions at every meeting: "How did you pick the vendor for the milk order?" "Why did you buy that brand of washing machine for the home economics classroom?" "Do you hire coaches who teach or teachers who coach?" "Why give teachers a 4% raise when the Consumer Price Index is only 2.8%?"

One evening the superintendent had finally had enough and openly attacked the elderly gentleman for meddling in school affairs and wasting important time.

"Don't you have anything better to do than attend board meetings and bother people?" he asked. "Why don't you take up a hobby like fishing and give the rest of us a break?"

Unfortunately, the superintendent found out too late that the elderly gentleman was a retired physician who indeed had nothing better to do with his time than study school district records and budgets. The school district, not fishing, became his hobby—one he pursued with renewed vigor after the superintendent spoke out. My friend's 20-second outburst of temper resulted in a continuing problem for him for several years.

My friend learned the hard way that anger solves few problems, and directly attacking the opposition almost never works.

■

Simplify, simplify, simplify

The other day I read in a professional journal that I had an impossible job. The article painted a dismal picture: increased political pressures on school officials, a barrage of negative media coverage of schools, and conflicting demands from a distrustful, antagonistic public. The article concluded that there was no way I could possibly be successful. I was doomed.

I didn't throw my hands up in despair, pull out the classified ads, and contemplate a quick career change, though I thought about it.

The world is indeed a complicated, complex place. There are lots of demands on public officials, and probably too many negative people receiving too much attention. But is my career as a school leader headed for the proverbial toilet?

I don't think so.

Whenever things get too complicated in life, I can hear Henry David Thoreau whispering in my ear: "Simplify, simplify, simplify." The more complex our lives and our jobs become the more important it becomes to isolate what is essential and basic to our success. That's a pretty short list — Focus on students and their learning; try to treat people fairly and honestly; don't spend more money than you have; admit when you are wrong; and be humble when success comes your way.

■

Solve problems as close to their point of origin as possible

A parent was in my office recently on more of a social than a professional call. She had three children who had graduated from our high school and I knew her quite well from ad hoc committee work and attending sports events. As she entered my office, she laughed nervously.

"I don't ever recall being in your office before. It's a little scary," she said. I could almost see her looking for the instruments of torture.

"It's a sad reality, Mary Beth, you have to be pretty desperate to walk through a superintendent's door," I laughed. "I'll assume you're not my typical client. I promise not to suspend, expel, or fire you."

Though I was smiling, the statement was true. The degree of the problems that walk through my door daily range from critical to terminal. The reality of the organizational chart is that I am the court of last resorts. My office is living proof that if you want to effectively solve problems, you deal with them at the lowest possible level in the system. As problems work their way through the system, the easy ones get solved and the impossible ones get passed along. If all of the problems in your system are allowed to rise to the top, you're in big trouble.

Your life can be made a little easier if you follow these four simple problem-solving rules:

1. Be sure problems are solved at their lowest point of origin. For instance, classroom management problems need to be solved at the school level. Minor facility problems need to be dealt with at the building level.

2. Be sure problems get solved efficiently. Taking too much time to solve minor problems only frustrates people and makes them cynical. People who take too much time to solve problems get by-passed. People will avoid them and target the best decision makers as they pole vault through the organization looking for a quick fix.

3. Be sure people know the process you use for solving problems and follow it. Don't let people automatically send their problems to you. If you have a chain of command, use it.

4. And, lastly, be sure there is integrity in your appeals system. If people automatically are told *No* on every issue, you have, in fact, no appeals system. You have to honestly look at each decision individually on its own merits.

79

■

Sometimes logic and bad weather just don't mix

I t's mid-January. The wind is blowing a driving snow and it's 10 degrees outside my office. The phone rings.

"Can I speak to the idiot who made the stupid decision not to cancel school today?" an angry voice asks.

"Yes, you may. I am that idiot," I reply.

"How could you jeopardize the safety of my children by sending them out in these inhumane weather conditions?"

I explain in great detail the multi-step, scientific approach we take to decide when to close school because of adverse weather. We contact local and state police for road conditions and the National Weather Bureau for an updated weather report and then we drive a select route within the district.

He isn't impressed.

"Don't you care about kids?" he inquires.

"Yes, I do care about kids. I have five of them and they are all in school this morning," I respond.

"I just don't understand how they could place a guy like you in charge who is obviously heartless. How can I appeal your lousy decision?"

"You have the ultimate appeal. If you don't like my decision, don't send your kids to school today. Exercise your authority as a parent and keep them home."

There is a long pause.

"I already have. They are home."

"Oh, really. And where are your kids right now?"

"In the backyard playing. You don't think I'm going to let them stay in the house all day long do you?"

When I try to explain that his children had already been exposed to the weather longer than if they had waited for their bus, he explodes.

"The blood of innocent children is on your hands," he barks and slams the receiver in my ear.

Logic doesn't work with some people. Engaging them in extended phone conversations isn't a productive use of your time. Your best option is to be polite, present your case, and then move on with the rest of your day. Hopefully, you will run into at least a few people who will appreciate your wisdom.

■

Speak a few reasonable words

A research study on what people most fear surprisingly reveals that the second most common fear is death. The first isn't snakes or an IRS audit; it's public speaking.

Our reputation as leaders is based on a relatively small amount of public information, and much of our image hinges on what we say in public. Yet many school leaders fail to do the necessary preparation to give thoughtful, coherent speeches and instead talk off the cuff. This approach usually leads to too much educational jargon and too many vague generalizations. We unwittingly appear disorganized and empty headed—hardly the image we want to convey.

Each of us has only a finite number of public contacts: board meetings, presentations to parent and community groups, graduation speeches, and so on. Every one is important.

Here's what you can do to create a positive, polished public appearance. Limit yourself to no more than two major ideas per speech or presentation. Focus on what your audience wants to hear or what they need to be told. Tell a story or anecdote to illustrate your major points. And unless you are a naturally gifted comic, leave humor to professional comedians.

Prepare a script for your speech or presentation and follow it. Then practice, practice, practice. Let someone you trust preview the speech for you. Then practice some more.

Give an advance copy of your script to key officials, board members, and the local papers. This should help minimize the number of times you are misquoted by the local papers and gives important people who can't hear you in person an accurate summary of what they missed.

Even if you give an occasional poor speech, audiences will at least appreciate that you thought enough of them to prepare your comments in advance.

Goethe tells us that "one ought, every day at least, to hear a little song, read a good poem, see a fine picture, and, if were possible, to speak a few reasonable words."

When your opportunity arrives, prepare yourself to speak as many reasonable words as possible.

■

That which does not kill us makes us stronger

As a high school principal, I had a staff member who delighted in publicly challenging everything I said and did, and always with a smile on his face. I could anticipate that he would greet any new idea or program with skepticism and resistance. To survive, I had to think through every option carefully before making a recommendation. People grew to believe I was one of the best organized principals of all time. They were wrong. I was merely responding in advance to the questions I thought I would be asked by my biggest critic.

We all need critics. They play a major role in helping us improve. Whether or not it was his intention, my favorite critic made me a better leader.

Nietzsche was right when he said, "That which does not kill us makes us stronger."

■

The only thing worse than telling your Board nothing is trying to tell them everything

As a novice superintendent, I thought there was a direct relationship between the amount of information I gave to the Board and good communication. I was wrong. Aristotle was right, when he said, "There is a balance to all things in life," including how much you try to communicate with your Board.

Volumes and volumes of information won't create a sense of trust or confidence, but can have the reverse effect and lead instead to cynicism and distrust. It can also generate pointed questions. Why are we getting so much information? Is this some kind of a plot to blind us with paper or confuse us? The larger the board packet, the more likely it will sit on the dining room table unread and get opened at the board table.

It's easy to fall into the dangerous habit of trying to provide major reports on every aspect of the district. This encourages board members to want to know every minute detail and blurs priorities. Without any focus to communications, everything looks important.

The solution is concise, well-timed reports. One-page executive summaries on key issues can give board members enough information to understand issues. Weekly phone calls can fill in the details and give board members the chance to ask follow-up questions.

You need to continually reinforce to board members that they don't have to know everything to be effective. Being a good board member is partly an act of faith; board members have to trust that daily operations and minor routine problems will be dealt with by their administrators. That is the message you most need to communicate.

█

The people you hire today will determine what your organization will be tomorrow

"**W**hy spend so much time and money hiring a new teacher?" he asked me. "The world is filled with teachers. They're a dime a dozen."

"Yes. The world is filled with teachers," I agreed. "And the world is filled with women, too. But I wouldn't hire every teacher or marry every woman. I prefer to be just a little bit selective."

How many schools or businesses spend as much time working with their best employees as they do working with their worst? Precious few. If you find yourself constantly focusing on your worst employees, you have lost focus. Hiring the best people is the single most powerful tool you have for improving your school district over the long run. If you spend your time, energy, and money on hiring the best people available, you can avoid spending all of your time trying to get rid of your mistakes.

We can all quickly calculate the approximate cost in time and energy of hiring a new employee, but have you ever considered the cost of hiring the wrong person? I would rather spend my time and money up-front hiring the right person than spend my time, energy, and money later on trying to get rid of the wrong person.

Employees collectively determine the future of an organization. Yet many of us treat the whole hiring process as an afterthought. In schools, we typically hire our new employees at the end of the school year after all of the "important" jobs are done. We create the impression that hiring the best people isn't a top priority, but something to fill up our summer months. And we foster the notion that we would rather spend money somewhere else in the organization.

A shrinking pool of teaching candidates in the near future should make all of us reconsider our priorities.

Here are 10 steps that should improve your chances of making the best possible decisions when hiring new employees:

Step 1: Put your money behind your priorities. Start by allocating 3-5% of your total budget for recruiting and training staff.

Step 2: Break the employment cycle. If you know you are going to have resignations and vacancies, why wait until the last minute? Interview and offer contracts in the fall for the next school year. The longer you delay, the more you will be forced to compete with everyone else for the best candidates.

Step 3: Make a conscious decision about where you want to be in 10 years and then hire people who can get you there. Create an employee profile that clearly spells out the skills and attitudes you expect from new employees. They are the engine that will drive your car.

Step 4: Create a marketable image for your school. Spend time and money on developing an "employment package" for candidates about your school. Include a job announcement, a profile of who you are looking for, school brochures, information on your community, and an application that looks different from everyone else's and also gets the kind of information you need to make good decisions.

Step 5: Expand your search. Go beyond the local colleges and universities. Add to your list all of the top teacher education programs and also colleges that turn out the largest number of candidates. Be sure to include historically black colleges and schools with sizable minority populations. Use the Internet to list all of your job openings.

Step 6: Actively court candidates. Target the top candidates in schools of education and begin to court them in their junior year. Identify the best teachers in area public and private schools and directly contact them.

Step 7: Train everyone involved in the hiring process and, in particular, staff members who serve on interview teams. This will raise the level of professionalism and ensure consistency throughout the system in hiring practices.

Step 8: Alter your interview process. Try to make your process reflect who you are. If you say you are a warm, caring organization, your process should reflect it. Avoid formal settings with predictable questions that will beg a "canned show." You want to hire the best person, not the best actor.

Step 9: Use your community. Have local residents form a welcome team to answer questions and take candidates on tours of the community.

Step 10: Once you have hired talent, develop it. Create a special training program for all first-year employees and assign them a mentor to ensure their success and protect your investment.

The truth lies somewhere between what our critics say and what we believe

It was my first major administrative post and I was more than a little proud and filled with myself. This was the big time. I had arrived.

I was to give my first speech at a joint meeting of the PTAs. The audience would probably be filled with mothers eager to hear my words of wisdom. The president of the PTA greeted me; she would do the introductions.

The auditorium filled. The PTA president diligently summarized my complete resume in flowery prose. It sounded like the second coming of Christ, only better. The moment had finally arrived: "And now ladies and gentleman, it is an honor to present to you, Dennis Kelly, our new stupid-intendent."

The audience sat in stunned silence. Then a large man in the rear began to snort through his nose. The snorting quickly became open laughter and then a clattering as people elbowed each other, guffawed, and tried not to fall off their folding chairs. This was not the welcome I had anticipated, not the beginning of my dreams.

There is mercifully no public record of the speech I gave that evening. The world quickly forgot my words; only my own repressed memories remain. And no one has been able to convince me that my introduction was unintentional and not a planned public humiliation.

I learned that night that we are given critics and lessons in humility in our lives so that we can retain some sense of reality about who we are and our real importance in the world. Left unchecked and unrestrained, our egos can destroy us. Occasionally, like trees, we need to be cut back and trimmed to size. This pruning allows us to still fit in the confines of our offices and promotes growth. It can also add a little fun and humor to a world and profession that desperately needs laughter.

■

There is no such thing as a small problem that involves someone else's money

I had just moved into a new district and was having lunch in a quaint Italian restaurant with a fellow superintendent from a neighboring district. He had his own private table and didn't need a menu to order. Everyone knew him by his first name.

"I eat here all the time," he told me. "I like to have administrative staff meetings here and treat the Board to dinner. I like the atmosphere and the food is great. It beats meeting in the boardroom anytime." When the bill came, he paid the tab with a school district credit card.

As we left the restaurant I couldn't help but share my concern. "Jack, should you be spending school district money on so many meals. Aren't you afraid of an audit or taxpayers going nuts?"

"Why are you worried? That's what money is for—to spend."

But I was right to be worried. A year later a major scandal surfaced in his district. All of the allegations focused on finances. The investigation eventually centered on my colleague and his use of school district funds. They never got to his lunch account. He was charged with falsifying his expense account to cover phantom moving expenses. He was tried and convicted. He lost his job, ruined his career, and even lost his pension, all for a few thousand dollars.

■

There will always be a right fielder on your team

I n elementary school, we played baseball during lunch hour. All of the kids would form a long line and two captains would choose us one by one for their teams. The last two kids picked were always banished to right field. They were non-players who, left to their own in right field, were more likely to pick flowers than chase fly balls. We figured if they batted last and no one ever hit a ball to them, how much damage could they really do?

Then we all grew up, and our adult lives now mimic our kids' games. How many of us has a non-player or two on our current team? What do we do with the weakest performers in our school district? Do we have our own special version of right field for them?

Many of us get frustrated trying to work with our weakest people. Nothing seems to help. Some of us try to ignore them, hoping they will resign or take early retirement. Others devote hundreds of hours trying to remediate their performance. Others hide their problems away in a library, study hall, or in a paper-pushing position. Too many of us, though, suffer from the delusion that banishing our weakest players to right field will somehow help strengthen the organization. It doesn't work that way.

The performance of students who are failing seldom goes from F to A overnight. They improve in small increments. So do adults. Too often we try to take our worst employee and overnight make him into a top performer. But real growth takes time.

What if you met with your problem employee and said, "Over the next 90 days I want you to improve your performance by one letter grade? Let's identify three things you can do to meet this goal.

Now what can I do to help support you?" This is a much different approach than developing a remedial plan with 20 items. And it will be more effective.

As any good baseball coach knows, it's best to help your right fielder learn how to hit singles and catch fly balls before working on a home run swing.

■

Treat the people in your organization like owners, not renters

One of my friends who is a realtor told me she could accurately predict the number of people in a neighborhood who owned their homes by the condition of their lawns and houses because homeowners take much better care of their property than renters. They cut the grass and touch up the paint. It is their property and an important investment.

You can apply the same principle to a school system. You can accurately predict the success of a school system by the number of employees who act like owners not renters.

"Renters" never fully commit to a system because they plan on being somewhere else in the future. They do what is legally required, but seldom go beyond the contract. They have very limited responsibility. They view their job simply as a way to pay the bills or add another line on their resume. They will not commit themselves to the district or anyone in it.

"Owners," on the other hand, make a long-term commitment to the school system and are emotionally attached. They speak of their job as a career and commit to a school as if it were a family unit. They are a loyal and important part of your school community. They take real pride in what they do and their performance shows it.

You need to make the people in your system feel like owners. This means involving them in decisions, giving them responsibilities, and expecting a commitment from them. It also means creating a family-like climate where good people can reasonably expect to spend their careers in one place.

■

Use your time and your staff wisely

I can still clearly remember my first administrative position. Each day my secretary would place a huge stack of mail on the corner of my desk. I was determined to read every piece carefully, even if it took half the day. Wasn't it my professional responsibility to read it?

In truth, I was more than a little paranoid. What would happen if I didn't read all of the mail and missed some critical piece of information? I could imagine missing a state report and losing funding, or not seeing the description of a new educational program and then being asking a question in public I couldn't answer.

So I poured through the mail until I read myself nearly blind. Then, with the help of a wiser, more experienced colleague, I got smart. One day he saw me crouched over a huge stack of mail and began making fun of me. He told me his secretary threw away half of his mail and he threw away the other half. When he finished laughing, he explained his system in more detail. When his secretary screened the mail each day, she separated it into four piles: (1) junk mail, which comprises about half of everyone's mail; (2) mail that should be directed to someone else's office; (3) mail to read and then discard; and (4) the important mail that should be read and remembered.

Each year over 50,000 books get printed in the United States, so even the most literate person in America can't read 1% of what is being published. The same holds true for your mail. The presses, publishers, and state departments of education will always be able to print it faster than you can read it.

You need to hire a great secretary, train him or her thoroughly, and trust him or her to make your job easier. Then sit back and relax a little. You don't have to know everything to be successful, which is a good thing, because you would go crazy trying.

■

When the going gets tough . . .

It's February again. For the 21st consecutive year, I have been told that staff morale has never been lower. If they think they are depressed, they ought to climb inside my head and see some real misery.

Being a leader can get pretty depressing. Your office can seem to have a magnetic force that draws only problems. It's easy to celebrate successes, but what do you do when things don't go well? People look to you for hope, for inspiration, for a smile during the worst of times. You are a personal barometer for your organization.

That's why you need to find a way to make yourself happy when things are bleak. Don't look to other people to make you happy, that's your responsibility. Learn how to whistle, sing, and smile during times of duress and distress. And while you are working on your outward show, work on your internal mental health. Cultivate positive friends and make a pact with them to take care of each other. Block off mental health afternoons during stressful times of the year and shut the door and read a favorite book or listen to a special CD for an hour. Go to the gym and work off some of your stress.

And, if all else fails, buy the biggest jar of Rolaids they sell and put it in your desk drawer. Offer them as breath mints to your friends.

■

You can't delegate compassion

The funeral home was almost empty. The father of one of my students had died unexpectedly. Just as unexpectedly I found myself uncomfortably sitting in a straight-back folding chair. Why was I there anyway? Couldn't I have just had my secretary send flowers or a note of condolence?

It was early fall and in a large high school, a kid like Jim Belanger didn't stand out. He was a less than average student who worked in the local gas station and spent most of his time fishing. His family lived in a shabby, rented house on a backwater canal near the lake. The death of Mr. Belanger wasn't going to make Jim's life any easier.

I finally decided as long as I was trapped in a funeral home on a Saturday night, I might as well try to do something positive. So I went up and began talking to Jim. We talked about the water level of the lake, fall fishing, stock car racing, who made the best pizza in town, and what he and his friends were planning to do after high school. And then we gradually began to talk about his father. What his father was like. Some of the best memories from their life together. The funniest thing his father ever did.

Our conversation lasted the rest of the evening and the rest of the year. Before the start of each school day, Jim would stop by my office and we would talk. In the process, he became a better student and I became a better person. I learned a great deal about listening and the value of silence when others need to talk.

Our friendship grew, and by the time Jim graduated from high school he was my favorite student. He eventually attended a community college, opened his own small business, and became a respected citizen, good father, and friend to others.

In thinking back to that evening in the funeral home, I sometimes wonder what I would have missed if I had just sent a floral arrangement? I have grown to realize that there is no substitute in life for caring and compassion, and it isn't something you can delegate to others.

■

A Final Note

One last lesson to learn. You don't have to leave people behind.

It's been fun reminiscing about my 20 years as a school administrator. The towns and the buildings have all blurred together, but the people remain clear and in focus. It's surprising how many people have been resurrected from the depths of my memory and now live again on the pages of this book. It's also been cheap therapy. Some of the agonies I thought I never would be able to forget or forgive I have now finally let go. Hemingway said, "For everything we leave behind in life, there is something we take away with us." I prefer to think that you can leave behind heartaches and mistakes and take away only the best memories.

During the Depression, my father started right out of high school unloading boxcars for an automotive company. He retired from the same company 42 years later. His was the last generation of "womb-to-tomb" workers. My career has been totally different. I suspect yours will be, too. If you are starting out as an administrator or plan to advance up the career ladder, get used to seeing a moving van in front of your house.

But as you leave for new jobs, you don't have to leave people behind. With recent advances in technology, it's easy to take friends and professional colleagues with you. Through e-mail and the Internet, you can maintain contact and continue to network with people from every phase of your career.

You might have finished reading this book, but you aren't quite done yet. I'd like to hear about your life as a leader in our schools.

AMERICAN ASSOCIATION OF SCHOOL ADMINISTRATORS

We all have at least one important story waiting to be told. What's yours? Do you have a story you would like to share with me to be included in a future book? If you do, e-mail me at dekelly@lths.w-cook.k12.il.us. I would also love to hear your comments and suggestions about what worked or didn't work for you in this book. I, too, still have a few more lessons to learn before I am done.

■

About the Author

Dennis Kelly is the superintendent of Lyons Township High School in La Grange, Illinois. He has taught preschool through graduate level and has been a department chair, high school principal, curriculum consultant, and educational researcher. He has five daughters and lives in the Western suburbs of Chicago.

■

AMERICAN ASSOCIATION OF SCHOOL ADMINISTRATORS